SAM[

M000078532

THE BOY WHO LISTENED

TOLD BY CARINE MACKENZIE
ILLUSTRATIONS BY FRED APPS

Samuel was a very special baby. His name meant, 'Asked of God.' His mother Hannah gave him that name because she had prayed for a long time for a son of her own.

When Hannah prayed for a child, she made a promise to God. 'If you will give me a baby boy,' she said, 'I will give him back to you to work for you all his life.'

God answered her prayer and soon Hannah and her husband Elkanah had a baby son. Hannah looked after her baby, and loved him dearly but she did not forget her promise to God.

So when Samuel was old enough, Hannah took him to the house of the Lord in Shiloh, where Eli was the priest. 'I prayed here for this son,' Hannah told him. 'The Lord gave me what I asked for. I am keeping my promise to God and returning my child to work for the Lord.'

Hannah and Elkanah made a visit once a year to the Temple to worship God in a special way. Hannah brought with her a new coat which she had made herself for Samuel. How she must have looked forward to these visits. And how pleased Samuel would have been to see his parents.

Young Samuel worked hard for God in the Temple. He learned to help old Eli with many tasks. Eli was pleased with his work.

God was also pleased with Samuel. He worshipped God and served him every day.

One evening, Eli who was nearly blind, went to bed as usual. After he had finished his evening work, young Samuel also went to bed. As he lay there, he suddenly heard a voice calling his name, 'Samuel.'

He thought, 'Eli must be wanting me.'

'Here I am,' he answered, as he ran through to Eli. 'You were calling me.'

'I did not call you,' said Eli. 'Go back to bed.'

Again he heard someone calling, 'Samuel!'

Again Samuel got up and went to Eli.

'Here I am,' he said. 'You did call me.'

'I did not call you,' said Eli. 'Lie down again.'

God was really calling Samuel but he did not realise it yet.

When Samuel went through to Eli for the third time old Eli knew that the voice Samuel was hearing was God's voice. He told him what to do. When God spoke to Samuel again, Samuel knew to reply, 'Speak, for your servant is listening.'

God told Samuel that Eli's sons were very wicked, and because Eli did not punish them the whole family would be punished.

Samuel lay in bed thinking about what had happened. In the morning he got up to open the doors of the Temple. He was afraid to tell Eli what God had told him, but Eli asked him what God's message was. 'Don't hide anything from me,' he said. After Samuel told him, Eli humbly said, 'He is the Lord; let him do what seems best to him.'

God was with Samuel as he grew up and guided him. The people realised that Samuel was a prophet who spoke God's words. All that he said was listened to carefully.

The country of Israel was in trouble. The Philistine army had defeated them, killing thousands of soldiers and even capturing the precious holy box, called the Ark of the Covenant, which should have been kept in the Temple.

The people of Israel were very sad because it seemed as if God had abandoned them.

Samuel the prophet gave them good advice, 'If you are serious about returning to the Lord, you must destroy all the idols and false gods that you have been worshipping. I will pray to the Lord for you.'

The people gathered with Samuel. They went without food to show that they were truly sorry for their sins.

When the Philistines heard that a great crowd of Israelite people had gathered, they decided to advance with the army against them. The Israelites were very afraid. 'Pray to God to save us,' they urged Samuel.

So Samuel offered a sacrifice to the Lord and prayed earnestly to God to help Israel. And he did. A huge thunderstorm broke. This alarmed and confused the enemy soldiers so much, that the Israelite army was able to chase them away.

Samuel erected a stone monument there to remind the people that God had helped them.

Samuel was a wise judge in Israel for many years. When he grew old, he retired and appointed his sons as judges in his place, but they were not like their father. They were greedy and accepted bribes. The people were not happy about it. 'Give us a king like the other countries round about,' they begged.

Samuel was very upset. He asked God what he should do. 'Do as they ask,' God replied. 'They are not just rejecting you, they are really turning away from me, but warn them what it will be like to have a king.'

So Samuel told the people how a king would want them to work for him in all sorts of ways and to give him a share of their crops and possessions. Yet the people still demanded a king.

Saul, a most handsome young man, was sent to search for some missing donkeys. He and his servant had no success and decided to ask for help from the famous prophet Samuel. When Samuel saw Saul coming towards him, the Lord told him, 'That is the man who will be the first king of Israel.'

Saul was the guest of honour at a special meal.
Samuel and Saul talked together well into the
night. The next morning Saul headed back for
home, but before he left, Samuel took a flask of oil
and poured it on Saul's head – this was the sign
that Saul was to be the king.

Saul did not carry out all of God's commands. He disobeyed him, choosing to please the people rather than God.

Samuel had the unpleasant job of facing up to Saul and telling him that God was displeased with him, and had rejected him as king.

Samuel's next task was to choose a new king – the young handsome David who loved and served the Lord.

Samuel loved and served God from his earliest years until his death. He was a man of faith – listening to God and speaking to him on behalf of the people.

Samuel spoke God's word – even when it was difficult.

God wants us to listen to him too and to obey his word to us, the Bible. He wants us to speak to him in prayer – asking him to forgive us for all our sin, through Jesus Christ.